My Innocent Mind Before Vietnam

BANANA

My Innocent Mind Before Vietnam
After Vietnam A True Story About PTSD

authorHOUSE®

AuthorHouse™
1663 Liberty Drive
Bloomington, IN 47403
www.authorhouse.com
Phone: 1-800-839-8640

© 2013 by Banana. All rights reserved.

No part of this book may be reproduced, stored in a retrieval system, or transmitted by any means without the written permission of the author.

Published by AuthorHouse   06/07/2013

ISBN: 978-1-4817-6177-2 (sc)
ISBN: 978-1-4817-6178-9 (e)

Library of Congress Control Number: 2013910530

Any people depicted in stock imagery provided by Thinkstock are models, and such images are being used for illustrative purposes only.
Certain stock imagery © Thinkstock.

This book is printed on acid-free paper.

Because of the dynamic nature of the Internet, any web addresses or links contained in this book may have changed since publication and may no longer be valid. The views expressed in this work are solely those of the author and do not necessarily reflect the views of the publisher, and the publisher hereby disclaims any responsibility for them.

Dedicated to PTSD victims,
My wife and family
And the U.S.A.

Introduction

This story is about a young man, myself, who was brought up in a loving, religious and very close family. This book talks about my humble beginnings in a rural village in Easter Maine. From there the book tells about how I gradually moved up in life until the day I was drafted (1969) and eventually ended up in Vietnam.

The main reason for this book is to make families aware of PTSD and how this problem controls your mind and you life. PTSD is a slow and very forceful controlling illness

PTSD is not an illness you want to let your mind get to much power over your life. The longer it has time to grow the more power PTSD has over your mind.

I truly hope this book will open the eyes of people on how war affects the minds of veterans and their families.

*A True Story on
PTSD
And
Mind
Control*

Early Life

My name is Terry, born in Lincoln, Maine December 26, 1947. I am one of five children, one brother and three sisters. Very Catholic, attended church every Sunday whatever the weather. We were very close with all our family and relatives.

Very early in my life we moved to rural eastern Maine. My dad worked for a farmer, getting $25 a week. We lived in the farmer's hired hand house. Consisted of four rooms and two bedrooms and two rooms downstairs. We had no indoor bathrooms it was outside in an outhouse and we had no running water indoors. We had to carry water from the stream. We had a wood stove and no refrigerator. Our food was placed in the nearby stream or placed in a root cellar. We ate very well because we had a cow for milk and made butter with the cream. We had pigs, chickens, large garden, etc. Mom cooked on the wood stove, baking bread, canning vegetables, etc. My mom had to wash clothes by hand with a washboard and iron clothes with a cast iron, which we heated on the stove. Even with all my moms work she always found time to come outside and play games with us. Dad, after supper, would get us all together and tell us stories that he made up. Every night it was a different story. Then we went to bed at 7 p.m.

Upstairs we had two rooms, mom and dad's bedroom, and our bedrooms. There were two beds separated by a sheet. I slept with my brother and my sisters slept together.

Before bedtime we all went to the outhouse because you didn't want to go outside at night because of the wild animals. Mom kept a slop pail inside just for emergency use only.

My school consisted of two rooms, one side consisted of 1st-6th and the other side consisted of 7th-12th. We did everything together, what a wonderful life.

I remember, we all were supposed to go to town Saturday, but the car had no heater. It was in the dead of winter and it was freezing. My dad said, "Don't worry I'll fix the heater." So we got water from the stream, and mom heated the water on the wood stove, so we all could take our baths. In the meantime, dad took the car to the farmer's barn to fix the heater. We were all cleaned up and ready to go. Dad finally came back with the car. He walked in with his head down and said he could not fix the heater. We were all disappointed. Dad turned around and said, don't look so sad, we're still going, so get ready. The only thing I need is some wood for the stove. We all thought dad wanted wood for the wood stove for the house, but the wood was for the car. Dad had taken the back seat out of the car and put a wood stove and a stovepipe into the window. He also put a small mattress for us to lie on. Dad put wood in the stove and off we went to town. Dad had only gone up to the 2nd grade, but was very ingenious when it came to thinking up stuff like that.

During potato picking season, school shut down and the whole family would go picking potatoes. We stayed at the farmers cabin for the length of the potato season. Picking potatoes was a hard a job but we always found time to play outside until bedtime. The bunks were on top of each other. The whole camp was one room. We all were in bed by 7p.m. dad would tell his famous bedtime stories and we all would say a prayer and off to sleep.

At the end of potato picking season, mom and dad would stock up for winter and buy clothes and shoes for school. The most money we made in one season was $999.00. We got paid 10 cents a barrel the first year. One barrel of potatoes took 6 to 7 baskets to fill. (Depending on the size of your basket)

The last time we went to pick potatoes, I was eleven years old. It was fun at the same time really hard work.

The clothes and a pair of shoes we got were for school only. When I would come home from school I took of my shoes and clothes. Most of the time, I would walk around barefooted.

I remember another time, thanksgiving was coming and we couldn't afford a turkey. Mom asked dad if maybe he could get a turkey from the farmer. Dad took the car and came back with 12 turkeys. Mom asked where did you get all those turkeys? Dads answer was they were walking along the roadside and he stopped and opened the back door and the trunk and they all jumped in. Nothing more was said.

One other time, mom asked dad if we all could go and visit with my grandfather. Pepe lived in Eagle Lake Maine and we now lived in Howland Maine. Dad said yes, even though we didn't have much money. Dad found away to save gas. When he got to the top of the hill, he would shut the car off and coast down the hill. Dad did this all the way from Howland to Eagle Lake.

My mom was forever working. She had an old pedal singer sewing machine. She made most of our clothes and the rest were hand me downs from my brother and sisters. We got a lot from our cousins. Mom would make quilts; hand-stitching pieces of scrape material. I tell you, when you got in bed you didn't move much because of the weight and also because they were so warm. During the night the wood stove would burn out. The only thing cold on your body was your face. Dad would get up around 4 a.m. in the morning and get the wood stove going. By the time we got up it was nice and warm. To this day, I don't know of any heat as warm and soothing heat from wood and the wonderful smell.

To this day, I can actually smell and taste the homemade bread and the homemade butter spread over a slice of bread. Mom also got up early in the morning and cooked a large breakfast.

One winter we were snowed in for over a week. Mom would have to crawl out the top window upstairs to go feed the animals, pick up the eggs and milk the cow. In one days time the snow had built up to the window. It would take a few days just to shovel a path to the outhouse and the shed where the animals were. We always had reserves of water in big boilers.

This life was simple and yet the most wonderful life for growing up as a kid. The closeness, the warmth, the complete dependability on one another. The love and respect for my parents was unspoken but was present everyday of their lives.

I wish, with all my heart, that I could return to this wonderful life. Money and material things have never made me feel the way I did in that little house with mom and dad in god's country.

The closeness I had with my cousins and uncles also changed. We use to spend all day Sundays, after church at each other's house. Mom and dad would play card and my cousins and I would play outside. We would share our hopes and dreams. If I only know now, what I didn't know than, I would have wished for my life to stay the same and never change. Our families remained close but nothing like it was as a kid. We ended up moving away for a better life. What a joke, we had the best life possible, (peace of mind).

Similar House

Four Rooms
2 rooms downstairs
&
2 rooms upstairs
Money cannot buy what we shared in this all house. Priceless!!

Life Changes

At the age of 5 we moved to Howland, Maine. Dad worked in the woods as a lumberjack and mom was always at home for us. This house had all the necessities indoor bathroom, lights, water, and a gas stove. The girls had their own bedroom and my brother and I had our own bedroom.

Life was good, but not like on the farm. We had to pay for the food, where as on the farm it was free.

We were still close but now we started having friends. We also got our first television and dad's story telling stopped. I really missed that part. Dad would only come home on weekends.

Mom was able to get an electric washer and a lot more conveniences. Dad got a better running car. We were moving up in life. Not always a good thing. Our relatives were further away and were unable to visit every week.

The move to Howland was made so we would have better schools and more opportunities. Each grade had its own room and teacher. Wow!

The biggest change was interaction with friends. That can be a good thing but at the same time can be bad. The environment, we were used to, life was predictable. We didn't expect much and we were content. Now I was hearing other kids problems, like wanting bikes, wanting to stay up later, bad mouthing mom and dad or sisters and brothers. These are simple issues but something my mind had to deal with even if they were not relevant in my life.

Another issue, which happened, was my brother's friends. They didn't want me to hang around with them. The worst thing happened as well, my brother went along with his friends. We had always played together and where you saw me, you saw my brother. This is another thing my mind was working on. What had changed so much for my brother to act this way? How could I get my brother back? Had I done something to bring about this change. The change in environment had already started changing how our family unit was starting to place more value on material things and friends. What a shame!

Another change was the school. Each grade had its own room and its own teacher.

The town had its own post office, one store, church, police station, and fire department. The population was approximately 1500.

We lived there until I was eleven years old. Than one day, while at school, our house caught on fire. We could see the fire and smoke coming through each end of the house from my school. The clock on the stove caused the fire and the damage was mostly smoke related. We were able to stay in the house but by the weekend, mom and dad had made up their minds to make another move.

My uncle, who lived in the city, had set up dad with a job and a nice rent.

Life had been good in Howland but I had experienced a different kind of life style. Material things were important now, money had become an issue with mom and dad and friends were replacing my sisters and brothers. The real closeness I had on the farm was never going to happen again. What a pity! On the farm we depended on each other to survive. The closeness and love was ever present. Money, friends, and material things could never replace what we had in that 4 room farmhouse.

Off to the big city. Wow!!

BHS

City Life

At the age of eleven, we moved to my present residence, Biddeford Maine. To me, this was a huge place with a population of over 20,000 people.

The schools were huge with many classrooms. They had a grammar school, a junior high, and a high school. All in different parts of the city. Every faith had their own church. That was unbelievable to me! The schools had job waiting for me when I graduate.

Moving on

Now, I am eighteen years old with a good jobs and my future ahead of me. I am a full time meat cutter at one of the largest chain of supermarkets in the state. I am making a great living and life is great.

I met a nice girl and I got engaged and was looking forward to getting married eventually.

I am still living at home. Things are kind of tight, money wise, so I help out at home. Money was not a problem with me and I was more than happy to help mom and dad.

Life is really great for my family and me. I did some partying with my fiancé we went to dances, movies, beach, and also family functions.

Work was more fun than a real job. The people were great and to think I got paid besides. I thought life was great and all my hopes and dreams were falling into place. I felt so lucky and happy. This crisis in Vietnam was heating up and the draft was rising. I am now 20 years old and I receive my draft notice in the mail. Not a problem, its my duty and I am ready to serve. I really love my job and my life but duty calls.

Learning How To Cut Meat

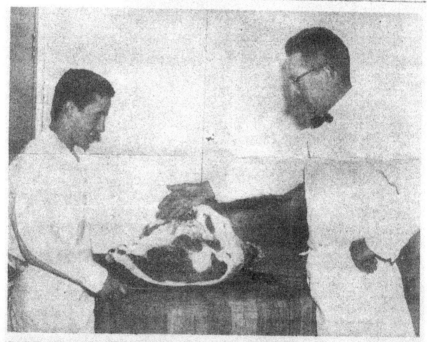

Biddeford-Saco Journal, Wednesday, June 9, 1965

LEARNING the meat cutting trade under the direction of Hubert Watson, meat manager at Russell's Shop 'n Save, Saco, is co-op student Terry Belanger of Biddeford High School. Belanger has completed such operations as boning, cutting steaks and roasts, hamburg grinding and has used such machines as bandsaws, tenderizers and grinders. Arrangement for this project was made through Richard Russell, manager.

Myself

LEARNING the meat cutting trade under the direction of Hubert Watson, meat manager at Russell's Shop 'n Save, Saco, is co-op student Terry Belanger of Biddeford High School. Belanger has completed such operations as boning, cutting steaks and roasts, hamburg grinding and has used such machines as bandsaws, tenderizers and grinders. Arrangement for this project was made through Richard Russell, manager.

My life changes forever

The day I got drafted was really scary and disappointing at the same time. My mom and dad were hurting for money and I felt responsible to help them. I had a good paying job as a meat cutter and was able to help with the finances.

On the other hand, I was also very scared about being drafted and the possibility of going to Vietnam.

My cousin had just been killed 2 months early by a land mine. He was just 18 years old. The funeral was so sad. He had a military funeral with the honor guard, taps, the folding of the flag to my aunt and uncle.

I tried to prepare for the day when I would leave and have to say goodbye to my family and friends. The day came and what a solemn and eerie feeling comes over you.

With the possibilities of ending up in Vietnam, and maybe not coming home alive.

I left for the army and was stationed at Fort Dix, New Jersey for 8 weeks basic training.

I never realized how bad people could treat other human beings. I was in good shape, weighing all of 115 pounds, but for those that were over weight, not so well. They were forced to do more exercises and in order to eat breakfast, lunch and supper you had to hand over hand bars before eating. If you didn't make it, you didn't eat. We had two really over weight guys in our company. I really felt bad for them. These guys at the end of six weeks lost so much weight they could not fit in their fatigue uniforms. At the end of the 6 weeks we were eligible for a weekend pass to go home. These 2 guys could not because they could no longer fit in their uniform. They spent the weekend doing exercises.

After basic training we went to AIT, which was training in the field you were going to perform while in the service. My training was in lightweight vehicle driver. Others were being trained for the infantry to serve in Vietnam. They got special training and were at another base.

At the end of AIT, I found out I was going to Vietnam. Before leaving for Vietnam I had ten day leave pass to go home.

When time came to leave from home I was ill and ended up at the Portsmouth Naval Hospital in New Hampshire. I had an in flamed stomach. It cleared up in a few days.

I left the hospital and returned to Fort Dix. I learned on arrival my unit had left for Vietnam. I was reassigned to an infantry in Vietnam.

The flight was long but not long enough. On landing in Cam Ranh Bay I met up with the guys from my unit who had been shipped over earlier. They were driving buses and were stationed in Cam Ranh Bay.

I learned I had been assigned to a military resupply unit in Chu Lai. I would spend 54 weeks at Chu Lai during the TET offensive.

The year was 1969-1970 and the TET. The last big push of force by the Vietnamese.

I took a Cargo Plane to Chu Lai where I waited to get picked up. While waiting to get picked up, I watched as guys were throwing bags on the back of a Chinook.

They were body bags! I had never seen a body bag, let alone seen bodies being handled that way. I got nauseous and began to vomit. I thought I was scared before but nothing like what I felt at that moment. I felt that this was going to be my ride home. "In a body bag."

Upon reaching my unit in Chu Lai, I got drunk. It didn't take much whiskey because I had never drunk alcohol in my life. I also never smoked cigarettes. I was so sick from the whiskey, that to this day, I can't stand the smell of whiskey.

I was there 2 weeks before I went on my first convoy. I drove a 2-½ ton truck filled with supplies to a firebase located off highway 1. Firebase would get incoming enemy action on a regular bases.

Before leaving with the Convoy, a sweep for mines was done in the morning. The sweep was done around 9 or so. We left the con fines of the compound and I drove down highway 1 with my shotgun, (another driver.) Approximately a half hour on Highway 1 the truck in front of me hit a mine and the driver went flying through the canvas roof of his truck and landed 50 feet or so into the rice patty. The last thing I saw was the guy being helped out of the rice patty. He seemed to be okay except for one of his legs. The convoy was forced to keep moving. The reason to keep moving was because the Viet Cong could key on our convoy and do more damage.

I had seen things like this on television but never thought I would be involved in such a vivid scene.

Needless to say, that incident was embedded in my mine every time I drove down Highway 1. Highway 1 was my only means of travel. I never drank or smoked cigarettes so much in my whole life.

Once we reached our destination with our supplies we hurried to get unloaded and get back into the convoy. The base we were resupplying would get fired upon almost every night. If the convoy did not form up by a certain time, it didn't leave until the next morning.

When I would get back from these convoys on highway 1, I drank to help numb the feelings and fear I was feeling. Not that this resolved what I was feeling because it didn't. It was a temporary mind numbing. I got into a mode of feeling numb from the danger of gunfire and the mines, due to the constant drinking.

Left to Right
Myself & Friend
The truck I hit the little girl with.

Deadly Card Game

The rear base was considered a pretty secure haven for guys coming to get some kind of rest and some good meals. This was usually for 3 days and then back into the field. The men who came to the rear were like brothers. They depended on each other for survival, as we all did.

How ever on this fatal night, a card game got out of hand and the worst thing possible happened. A dispute erupted over the card game and these two best friends got into a fight and one of them ended up getting stabbed and killed. This all happened just two tents down from mine. The incident was recorded as being killed in action.

There was no real safe place in Vietnam. The stresses of being in an unsafe environment can only be restrained for a while and than the mind snaps.

The young man involved in the confrontation was sent back into the field. Everything was kept quiet and no investigation was done, as far as I know.

Occurrences like this were not always recorded. War has a way of covering up these incidences and leading you to believe that these are the casualties of war. What a bunch of bull!

This was a human life with a family, friends and someone who gave his life in service to his country. The truth and justice is always the road to use.

This young mans life was not justly taken care of properly. The other man involved if alive, is still dealing with this episode in his mind.

Machete

Volunteering—What a mistake

Another one of my big mistakes was volunteering to help support Hill Center until reinforcements could be brought in. The TET offensive was in full force and this was the last big push for the Vietnamese.

I was a truck driver, not an infantryman. I had no jungle like training. I got on a Chinook, with three of my buddies and headed for the hill. It took about ½ hour before we reach this base on top of a hill.

I was only supposed to be on the hill for 3 days instead of 10 days. The pictures show myself and my buddies and the conditions we had to deal with while on the hill. The Chinook we came in on and helicopter we used for enemy drop offs. They also show us setting up glamour's to help secure our perimeter before nightfall.

It rained constantly while on the hill. We slept in two man tents in the mud. We had to sleep with our weapons inside next to us to help keep them dry.

The nights were so dark you couldn't see your fingers in front of your face. This had to be the scariest feeling I have ever felt in my life. If you smoked a cigarette, you had to hide the tip of the cigarette because the lit ash could be seen a long distant. Need less to say, I didn't smoke at night.

The nights were so quiet, to quiet. In order to try to keep the Vietnamese away from the hill, flares were shot into the air at midnight. This was called mad minute and everyone would shoot their weapons for a minute. I don't remember sleeping for more than 10-15 minutes at a time.

This is an aerial view from the rear of the Chinook as we left Chu Lai headed for Hill Center

Aerial view of Hill Center

Aerial view right before landing on Hill Center

My living accommodations for ten days. A two man tent.

Another picture of myself next to my tent.

Picture of myself & another driver from my unit.
The monsoon season was in full swing.

My tent was located just below this bunker. I was located
just below this large gun and situated right on the perimeter.

Setting up glamours for the night.

This picture depicts the helicopter used to drop off 2 enemy soldiers who refused to speak. They were dropped off in the air.

During one of these episodes the Captain, in charge, was shot and killed from friendly fire. They found the captain the next morning. It was proven the shot came from friendly fire at mad minute. They didn't find out who did it. The man had a wife and children back in the states.

The troops stationed on the "hill" disliked him a lot. Our one and only formation my friends attended, the Captain wanted us to spit shine our boots. We slept in the mud!! There was no way we could do this. I don't believe anyone deserved what happened to him.

I had only met him once at the formation but I couldn't believe things like this were possible among our own people. Shame on war.

I witnessed the mistreatment of several Vietcong whom I saw being kicked, beaten because they refused to reveal any information & were taken by helicopter and dropped to their deaths.

This kind of senseless violence by our own people was unbelievable to me.

While I was on the "hill", I visited one of the houches covered with sand bags. I could not believe what I saw. The entire place was covered in smoke from marijuana. Tables had pills spread around and alcohol was plentiful. This was all going on during the day. Knowing that come nighttime, these same people would be guarding the perimeter of the "hill", that really made me insecure and frightened for my life. I left the "hill" after spending ten days with no sleep, very little food, and completely soaked to the bone.

The day came for me to leave this hellhole and return to my home unit in Chu Lai. On leaving the hill we encountered in coming fire on the Chinook. Chinooks don't fly high quickly and are good target before they reach a fairly safe height.

The Chinook was filled with other personal as well as myself and the other truck drivers I went up with. I thought we had made it safely when we landed in Chu Lai with no injuries from the incoming fire from the "hill". Nothing could have been further from the truth. The incoming fire had killed a black sergeant. When someone went to touch him, the soldier fell forward, he had been hit by the incoming fire and killed. He was headed home from Chu Lai, so his fellow soldiers told everyone.

The picture below shows what condition I was in on returning to my home unit in Chu Lai.

My first thought as I landed was to show thanks.

Back at my home base. Still in shock after all the goings on Hill Center

The Silent Killer

Agent Orange was an ever present source of death. The chemicals in Agent Orange would kill all the foliage in the area. But our government told us that it would not harm humans. Not so, there are 17 different illnesses cause by Agent Orange. I received, by accident, papers from Washington D.C. which shows areas sprayed and the amount sprayed in Chu Lai. I got sprayed every morning for a long period by planes. A wet mist from Agent Orange covered my clothes. Agent Orange was safe for humans and only killed Foliage. What a joke. Did the government thing we were really that stupid?

I was really hurt and disillusions that are government, knowingly, would do that to our troops and me. Agent Orange is a slow death sentence.

I believe, I am one of the lucky ones who was not affected so far, by Agent Orange. They find knew illnesses all the time caused by Agent Orange.

On the road again

After coming back from the "hill" I got a few days off to try to rest and clean up. The next time I went out on highway 1, I was one of 3 trucks from my unit. I have to mention this before I go on. I knew very few of the real names of the soldiers I lived with for a year, here are some of the names:

Myself—Cherry boy—cowboy—red, Ras, Cox, Farmer, Frenchy, Studman, Casie, Fink, Cookie, Mack, Reb, Boss, and Cap. I really didn't want to know their real name incase something would happen to them. Not knowing can sometime be better than knowing.

Back to the 3 truck convoy on highway 1. We were unable to hook up with the larger convoy in the morning. We set out again on roads that probably were mined. I never knew if today was the day my luck would run out. On the way to the firebase I was supplying, I saw bodies of families who had been killed and left to rot away on highway 1. This was a scare tactic for the surrounding villages to not help the Americans or else.

That night we had to stay at the firebase because I had got there to late, so we had to spend the night.

I parked my truck near the helicopter pad and spent the night in my truck with my weapon. That was a big mistake. That night we got incoming fire and the choppers were in and out bringing in wounded soldiers. What a sight, bloody bodies some with arms and legs missing. Horrible. As bodies came in they were tagging their toes or foot. I later found out that the tags determined weather they were able to help them. If not, than you were giving a shot to help relieve the pain until their passing. The morning could not come fast enough. Almost every experience I had in Vietnam was something out of a real movie. The only thing was, this was not a movie and the people dying were not actors. The only movie is in my mind and it keeps playing. The same movie over, and over, and over again. You would thing your mind would get sick of playing the same thing over again. Well, guess what, my mind is still on reruns.

The morning came and I lined up my truck in the convoy. We waited for the roads to be swept for mines and than the convoy was allowed to leave. I got back to our unit safely but not without another lasting memory embedded in my mind. I didn't think it was possible to have so many memories in my mind and still be able to think clearly. Well, I found out its really not possible at times.

I went out one more time and this would be my last time before leaving Chu Lai. The guys needed supplies and we attempted to bring them but one of the bridges had been blown up and I was forced to turn back. What an awful feeling, not being able to help your fellow soldier. My mind was racing with the thought of the guys running out of ammo. Lucky when I got back to base, the Chinook was able to fly and they brought in supplies.

Life Savers

Chinooks

The Final days

My last 2 weeks in Chu Lai, I spent inside the compound. I made the ration run in the morning and helped out on guard duty at night. Sleeping was not at the top of my list. I had made it this far and I was not about to sleep and rely on someone else with my life. I caught one guy sleeping on guard duty and when I woke him up, he pulled a knife on me. I told him to put it away or I'd bury him where he slept. I had 2 days left, I told the warrant officer, and I was all done pulling guard duty. I didn't turn the soldier into my warrant officer.

I spent the last days saying bye to my Vietnam family. To be so close to people who helped keep you alive is beyond words. The camaraderie I had with these soldiers is something I have never experienced since and probably never will again.

The day has arrived and I can't believe I made it. God must have needed me somewhere. I felt guilty having to leave my family behind with all the dangers surrounding them. Happiness and guilt are powerful forces and I find them very hard to deal with.

I boarded and left Chu Lai and headed for Cam Ranh Bay. I was in Cam Ranh Bay for one more day and than back to the good old USA.

I thought I had left Vietnam behind; boy was I in for a rude awaking. My body came home but my mind and heart stayed in Vietnam

My Innocent Mind Before Vietnam

Landscape as I leave Chu Lai

A changed Mind

I landed in Fort Lewis and was there for 3 days. I went throw various tests. Nothing was mentioned about PTSD. Hex, PTSD wasn't heard of until the eighties, I believe. Years ago it was called "shell Shock".

While boarding the buses out of Fort Lewis we had demonstrators protesting the Vietnam War. I was welcomed home by having someone spit on me. Gee thanks!

Once I got to the airport, I took of my uniform and never wore it again. That part of my life was over, dead and buried. That's a joke!

I boarded the plane and headed for Boston. Upon Landing, my family picked me up at the airport. I didn't say much, especially about Vietnam. On arriving in Biddeford, I stopped at St. Joseph Church and said a prayer for all my comrades I left in Vietnam. I also asked god to try to forgive me for my faults and wrong doing in Vietnam. I've always felt guilt and shame about what I let occur and didn't try to help correct certain situations.

I arrive at home, sweet home and open the door and my little poodle was so excited she peed all over my shoes. I was happy and yet sad at being home. What a word home. Home meant this to me, family, friends, church, work and above all safety and peace.

The 1st night at home, I couldn't sleep. I dosed off for a few minutes and was awakened by a siren. When I realized where I was, at home, I was under my bed. The sleepless nights continue along with night sweats and my continuing movies in my mind about Chu Lai. I figured these would subside as time went on. No so!

I was twenty-one, strong and capable to handle any situations.

I reported to work after only a week. I wanted to get on with my life. I did something I had never done. I started to pretend to feel and be happy. I never acknowledge I was in Vietnam because I didn't want to explain or deal with that part of my life. The shame and guilt was starting to influence my actions. I was more cautious, quiet and not wanting to show any kind of connection with Vietnam.

I met my wife in 1970 and got engaged in 2 months. She is the reason I am still alive. We got married in 1972. I didn't discuss my experiences in Vietnam, so it was easy to cover up my problems.

When my daughter was born in February of 1974 my wall, around me, started to crack and eventually my wall crumbled. For months I could not hold my daughter, not knowing why because I love kids. I didn't make the connection with the little girl I hit in Vietnam.

I couldn't feel the joy and happiness, which my mind told me I should feel. I really felt a lot of guilt and shame for my attitude. Pretending was my way out. Shortly there after, I had dramatic surge in my recollection of the little girl. I started having serious stomach problems, trouble sleeping and night sweats. I became sleepless and experienced sexual trouble with my wife because of the intrusive thoughts and flashbacks to the episodes in Vietnam.

About the same time, I became meat manager at a large grocery store. I was replacing the man who helped train me. He was sent to another store within the same company. I had been betrayed again. The company told me he had chosen to make the move. I really felt guilty, after finding out, he was told to make the move.

My mind could not process and handle everything. The rise in flashbacks and other Vietnam related traumatic experiences caused my mind to shut down. I had a nervous breakdown and I was hospitalized with anxiety, crying spells, stomach pains and signs of acute nervous breakdown.

I was placed on tranquilizers and it took me 6 months to recover from these episodes. I could not understand what was happening to me and what was my problem. I was in my twenties, great wife, had a new baby and a good paying job. Life should have been great but not according to my mind. Thoughts of suicide were ever present in my mind. My mind was stuck in Vietnam and was getting increasingly worse. My loving wife is the one who got help for me and helped pull me and my mind out of a depressing situation. I was still not aware of PTSD.

Life became a daily struggle, but eventually I returned back to work. The man, whom I had replaced, came back as meat manager and I became his 1st meat cutter.

To help alleviate my stress, my wife took over the finances. My mind was incapable of handling to many things at once.

In 1975, I got a job for the U.S. postal service. I thought my mind had recovered from my episodes. Not so, I again experienced sleepiness and there were problems at work, which had nothing to do with me.

My mind was persistent and would not let go of Vietnam.

I used up a lot of sick leave and annual leave because of headaches, stomachaches, flashbacks, and anxiety. I began distancing myself from people as the episodes became more frequent.

The older I got, the harder the pretending became. Over a certain amount of time, my mind needed a break and this was when I used either sick leave or annual leave. At first it would take a day and as my age progressed I was using up to three days. This went on for years. I became more like a hermit, not going out unless I really had to, for example: family functions, funerals or special occasions. I would go and leave early. My mind kept me from letting me feel, but my mind was gracious enough to let me pretend to feel. My mind had made up its mind there was no room for more hurt.

My big problem was heavy rain. I would be up all night, reliving my all night movie theater in my mind. When daylight came, my mind was exhauster, and so was my body. My supervisor confronted me. He wanted to know why I took time of when it rained. I didn't go into detail but let him know I had no control over what was happening.

Years went by and than things came to ahead again. A Filipino man was being introduced to the work force. My mind quickly switched over to Vietnam and I became very upset and anxiety and I could not function. My mind was stuck in the episode where the Viet

Cong were being kicked and tortured. I had to leave immediately and did not return for another 6 weeks. The man was not hired in our office. I felt guilty, because it was my fault. This all happened in 1991. By this time, PTSD was known.

My supervisor referred me to the Vet Center for counseling in Portland. I met with a counselor, who also was a Vietnam Vet. I was beside myself with the thought of having to talk about my Vietnam experiences. I became teary eyed and had a hard time to speak. He put me at ease, and than proceeded to tell my problem, PTSD. I had never heard about PTSD until than. Over 20 years of hell, not knowing, thoughts of suicide, losing my mind. It was good finding out but it didn't begin to solve my problems.

I attended group counseling for over 3 years. My mind was having a real hard time dealing with my experiences without having to deal with someone else's experiences. After all these years (20) I was able to talk about the little girl I ran over in Chu Lai. I left the center this night and my mind was stuck and would not let go of that fatal scene. When I came to my senses, I was in another city and had to turn back to get home. That was the last time I went to group counseling.

The counselor sent me to Togus to see a VA doctor. I was not prepared or willing to tell him about the little girl because of my shame and guilt. The doctors diagnose was PTSD. This was the first time I was acknowledged as having PTSD. But the VA would not respect the doctor's findings. The reason being I had no evidence of being in a war zone. I thought Vietnam was a war zone. Boy, was that a shock to my mind. My mind was working overtime, all these years; only to find out I was not in a war!! I was denied any medical help or compensation. Now my mind was really pissed off. I was not about to let them get away with their decision. I went to Vietnam in a good faith. I got to Vietnam a whole man and came back in pieces.

I went back to work for the U.S. Postal Service after 6 weeks. I wanted to move up, so I took courses for supervisory positions. I was finalist on three separate postings. The last position I applied, I was denied because my sick leave record was bad. They did ask if I would help to train the man who got the position over me. I nearly lost it, but my mind said it was not worth it. I never applied for another postal position.

I went to see a VA doctor, he also diagnosed my problem as Post Traumatic Stress Disorder, delayed, and moderate in severity. I put in another claim to the VA for medical help and compensation. This was denied by Togus and also Washington D.C. At one point my claim went from Togus to Washington from Washington to Togus. This went on for over a year. Each time asking for records or additional information on my claim. I didn't have combat records or anything else. I didn't think, I was supposed to carry a notebook and write everything down with names and dates. I thought it was the government's job to handle that part of the war.

The point is don't give up on yourself and certainly don't let the government push you and your family aside.

At this time I would like for you to read how PTSD affected my family. The letters were written on behalf on my claim to the Veterans Administration in Togus.

This letter is from my sister and is written word for word.

Nov. 3, 2006

"This letter is on behalf of my brother. Terry Belanger. Since his time spent in Vietnam fulfilling his military obligation in the 1960's,

Terry has had periodic episodes of depression requiring medication so that he can function with his activity of daily living.

Terry was mostly fun loving before leaving home for the military but returned to us very sullen and at times very drawn. During the happiest times of his life, like the birth of his first child, he became almost reclusive and cried inconsolably for days and weeks. He didn't know what was wrong and we didn't know what to say or do to get him out of his depression. With the gentle and loving coping of his newly wed wife he sought out treatment and was put on medication.

Through the years, besides these bouts of depression, Terry developed epigastria problems secondary to the stress of not returning to his "normal self" before his sent in Vietnam.

Terry has spent his life going back and forth to the VA Center going through testing to diagnose and treat his presenting GI problems to no avail. Finally, his family MD needed to put him on antibiotics for an upper respiratory infection and his symptoms subsided and he was almost joyous of not being in pain anymore. This to was short lived and his symptom returned and persists even today. He cannot view the news or see a movie dealing with war as the Saudi War, Iraq War or the movie Pearl Harbor without going into a state of depression.

Terry will never be the same and, despite his efforts to be compensated for what the military did to him. The government he served robbed him of a happier life and their denial of the link they had on his life-long symptoms robs him of the truth. The government needs to walk in Terry's and our shoes to understand the effect this has had on our peace—loving brother.

On behalf of my brother, I ask for humane judgment on his behalf. He did his duty (a life—long—one) and now you, in a good conscience, should compensate him for his damaged life."

My daughter wrote the second letter.

Feb. 18, 2008

"My dads experience in Vietnam is still a mystery to me. Over the years I've learned bits and pieced about his terrifying past but not enough to tell the story. Conversations of the events in Vietnam has always been a hush, hush subject. I will never know the details of my dad's traumatic event, but I have observed how this has affected his battle—scarred life.

My dad seems so hopeless at times, not able to push all the bad thoughts out of his mind. He has a blank glare in his eyes, like he is emotionally numb. I know he blames himself for some of the things that happened in Vietnam and has a lot of guilt; which has a great affect on his well being. He gets depressed and detaches himself from people. At other times he can be very irritable, jumpy. He has out burst of anger, taking it out on others. He can be very abrupt and not get along with people. He's like night and day.

My dad avoids activities, movies, people or any reminders of Vietnam. Reminders of the events or certain triggers seem to cause more problems. For as long as I can remember, he has had a lot of stomach problems. He can't digest a lot of foods, vomits often, and has severe heartburn. He eats in one day, what I eat in one meal.

Since I was a child, I can't remember one night that my dad slept without interruptions. At night I constantly hear him pacing, watching television or the front door opening and closing. He never is able to relax, without having flashbacks or nightmares of the horrifying images of what happened.

For all the things my dad has done for me, my one wish for him would be to feel normal again and forget this catastrophic life experience."

My daughter only learned of the episode with the little girl I hit just two years ago. (2007) I didn't want to see her eyes when I told her about the incident. I was harboring enough shame and guilt and I certainly didn't want her to see that side of me. I thought I would wait until she was old enough to maybe better understand how these experiences were controlling my mind and my life.

The next letter is from my lovable wife. The love of my life and the reason I am still here. I really cannot understand why she would deal with a very broke man who is here one minute and gone to Vietnam the next. It must be love. My wife, who has really been there by my side threw it all.

Nov. 4, 2006

"34 years ago, I married a wonderful man, Terry. He is kind, loving and would do anything for those he loves. Two years after we were married he had a depression. He would not open up to me and tried to deal with it by himself. I had never dealt with this illness and I figured after a few weeks, he'd come out of it. Well it did not happen. If we had company he would go to another room and close the door. He avoided even his friends and family. I felt helpless, whatever I said or did, I could not get through to him.

Our daughter was 6 months old at the time. She needed her father's affection and I wanted my husband back. He finally agreed to seek help. While he was still struggling with depression we came across an article about Agent Orange. He went to the Veterans hospital in Togus. Agent Orange was not present. He has symptoms of PTSD but was diagnosed for PTSD much later in his life.

He had severe depression and had a hard time dealing with the fears through the nights. Vietnam did a lot of damage to my husbands mind and well being. Things you never forget like when he came home and people were spitting on him. There he was drafted into this war risked his life and got repaid by having people act like he was a criminal. That's a lot for a person to handle.

A lot of times, he doesn't want to go anywhere with me. He would rather stay home, it is safer and he doesn't have to pretend in front of others. Nights are the worst; he has a lot of nightmares and flashbacks from the war.

He has always been a good father to our daughter and she has been so good to her father.

I have learned to be patient and give my husband his space to a certain limit. I don't try to control or nag him and I think he respects me for it. Sometimes I look at him when he's depressed and down and see this wonderful man that came home from the war and left part of his soul in Vietnam."

This letter made me realize how much PTSD has damaged their lives as well as mine. I brought everybody I cared about aboard my ship, which had a big hole in it. My boat was sinking and I was bringing all the people I cared about down with me. Now my mind has more guilt to deal with. Is it possible for my mind to handle more guilt and shame?

Left to Right
Myself
Granddaughter
Daughter
Wife.

Cause and Effect of Environment

I found that my environment, often times would determine the kind of day I was going to have. If I saw an oriental person, helicopter flying overhead, planes, something mention in conversation, TV advertisements, Newspaper articles, bodies covered up, war, natural disasters, "911", and the list goes on.

All these things can trigger my mind to go off to Vietnam You cant control your environment, no more than I can control my mind.

I think the only way to control my mind would be to drug it. To the point, that my mind is not aware and in a numb state.

I am sorry, but to me that is worse than dealing with your mind and what direction your mind takes you and your body. I do try to limit my mind to things that are more safe and bearable. I don't go out, unless necessary. If I do go out, I know what I need, and get it and leave.

I enjoy cooking, I play cards either on my computer or not. I cut my lawn when everyone is at work. I do crossword puzzles. I go out to eat on special occasions and when I do, I look for the closest exit and a table situation where my back is against the wall and I am facing my exit. When I do go out with my wife, she does the driving.

Every once in awhile, I get in a situation that could not possibly happen but it does.

I was 55 years old and had just retired from the U.S. Postal Service in 2003. In August of 2003, I was driving my van and a little oriental girl ran in front of my vehicle. I came close to hitting her, my heart felt like it was going to come out of my chest. I stopped and my mind was headed for Vietnam again. She looked so much like that little girl, I couldn't let go of the image and my mind was stuck. The little girl ran of and I didn't see her again. But my mind would not let go of the image of that girl. I spent the weekend of Labor Day with extremely strong nightmares and my heart was pounding in my chest. My blood pressure skyrocketed and body mind could not relax. I spent the next two nights, up all night. I have two toy poodles and they stayed by my side through it all. On the second day, my daughter, who is a registered nurse, checked my blood pressure. She checked it for the next hour and told me if my blood pressure didn't come down I would have to go to the hospital. My blood pressure slowly started to drop. As far as my mind letting go, it didn't happen.

I ended up at the Vet Center in Portland. There I met a man who would help me greatly. He also had me see the staff Psychiatrist, who was a lady. I was crying and very nervous and not in control of much of anything. She prescript some medication for PTSD. This was the first time I was treated for Post Traumatic Stress Disorder. The year is 2003 and I have been dealing with PTSD for over 23 years. I should say, my family was also dealing with PTSD for 23 years.

I started seeing my present counselor and another Psychiatrist who is also my present caretaker. I made it known, I didn't want to be drugged to the point of being in a numb state. My doctor understood and I really respect these two men. The medication helped my body to relax. It didn't change the mode of my mind. I told the doctor, I would rather be aware of my surrounding and deal with my problems on a daily bases.

I have been seeing these two men for over 6 years. I see my counselor every month and I see my Psychiatrist also every month.

In between visits, I would see the little girl I almost hit at one of the stores and my mind take over and I had to leave the store immediately without picking up what I needed. I stayed in my Van for more than an hour until my mind released the rest of my body to leave. PTSD is all about my mind taking over and my inability to stop it. This may not be true for everyone but it is for me. We have so many more Orientals in America today than ever before. I don't have a problem with Orientals but my mind does. The image does not involve every little oriental girl. She has to have a certain look.

I am now 61, soon to be 62, and I still cannot control my mind completely where Vietnam and my environment are concerned.

After retiring from the Post Office, at age 55, I went to work as a meat cutter for a small market. The money was good and the hours were also good. My mind could not deal with my environment and its uncertainness. I find, as I get older, I need more stability and structure. I stayed at the market for six weeks and than gave two weeks notice. It's really disappointing when your mind can take over your life.

My Last Day!! 30 yrs.

Power of Politics:

Throw out the years; I tired to get help from some high profile political leaders. The response I got was they would look into my case.

Another agency said they were unable to perform the extensive research requested due to staffing and budget limitations.

Another political agency response was "it was not within their Jurisdiction."

A lot of these political leaders forgot who got them elected in the first place, I had made up my mind and I was not going to give up.

I wrote to congressman T.A. and immediately he answered my letter, personally he put his staff to work and within days the VA found 4,500 pages of combat situations of my unit in Vietnam.

The result was after 38 years, I was approved for PTSD and I was compensated from 1988 to present.

The point is, I never gave up, just like my family never gave up on me. My family and I will be forever grateful to Congressman T.A. and his staff.

Just to think that these papers were there all this time (38 years) and someone was too lazy to look for them. How many other poor victims go without medical treatment because someone behind a desk is too lazy to search for records. My life might have been different if I had received proper treatment after leaving the service in 1970.

PTSD and mind control are life altering problems and need to be dealt within it earliest stages.

Without this lady!! (My Wife)
I would not be alive today.

Never Ending Struggle

I found a job driving a school bus. I really enjoy being with the kids. I have kids from kindergarten, primary, middle and high school. I have been driving for over 5 years.

Towards the end of the school year in 2008, I picked up a kindergarten kid who was oriental and our eyes met. My mind went into shock and for a split second I was back in Chu Lai. I tried to place her in a safe seat, right behind mine. Two reasons, one she was safe and two I couldn't see her. At the end of the school year, I was left with a major problem. Whether to return the following year. My mind worked overtime during the summer trying to make a decision. I kept hoping she would not be on my bus. I discussed this with my wife and she left it up to me. I went to see my Psychiatrist and counselor and asked them to help me make a decision. But my mind would make that decision for me.

It's so nice to have a boss (your mine), which is one of the smallest parts of your body but has so much power.

I did decide to go back and the young lady was at the same bus stop. My mind is still processing the situation. I never know what's in store in the coming years. All I can do is let my mind handle it, the best way It can.

Help Finally!

Early this year (2009) Congress passed a bill having to do with PTSD. Under this anyone diagnosed with PTSD will be recognized and be rated accordingly. You don't have to show any documentation other that the doctors diagnosis. That means help is available immediately. When soldiers return home. Take advantage of the counseling. PTSD is nothing your mind can shut down. You maybe young and strong but your mind rules. To all you families with soldiers coming home with notice able changes, get help for them. Don't wait! Some signs of PTSD

Parents, wives, husbands who have soldiers coming back from any war, you want to notice these signs: some of the effects and signs present are quite noticeable. Socially different, quiet, unwilling to discuss his tour of duty or what happened in the war, sleeping problems, night sweats, crying secretly, wanting to be alone, looking into space with a blank look, avoiding family and friends. Staying away from crowds, family functions.

The other side is also noticeable. The happy go lucky and full of fun can also be a sign. This maybe just an act to draw attention away from having to deal with situations in the war. I know about these signs, because I did all of them at one time or another. Pretending is one of the roads I used most of my life (40 years).

The sooner you recognize these signs and seek help, the better your chances are, I hope, on having a fairly normal life. Never ending struggle!!

The Persuasive Mind!!

Your mind will make you think at times everything is fine. Don't be deceived, it's not fine where PTSD is concerned.

PTSD is a slow, disruptive and uncaring illness. It will suck-up all the good things in your life, like Family, Friends and the ability to truly FEEL.

I am now 63 years old and after 41 years of dealing with PTSD, I can only hope that you Young People can get the necessary help.

You want enough help to be able to be comfortable within Your Mind.

Please! Please! Please! Get Help!!!!!!

The End and Hope for a New Beginning For You.

About the Author

The author is a novice in the field of writing but was compelled to tell his story in order to help our men and women suffering from PTSD. Terry was a naive young man before he was drafted and came home as he states "in pieces" and those pieces are still together to this day.

Terry has battled many days of depression and yet held onto life despite the horrible visions of experiences in Vietnam. Through all his struggles, Terry has been a caring and giving person to his peers, friends, family and co workers. Over the years, Terry has internalized his struggles which has taken a toll on his body and caused withdrawals from his surroundings.

On the surface you find a jovial person who is driven to finish what he starts and to follow through on his given word. He strives to right the wrongs he sees daily. Though he feels taken over by the effects of Vietnam. It has made him a strong character to deal with and can usually get to the heart of any issues. He never gives up!!!

CPSIA information can be obtained
at www.ICGtesting.com
Printed in the USA
FFHW021040021019
55348878-61081FF